PAPER HOUSE

paper house

REBECCA BRENNER

WAYFARER BOOKS
ABIQUIU, NEW MEXICO

WWW.WAYFARERBOOKS.ORG

Published in 2025 by Wayfarer Books
Cover Design and Interior Design
by Connor Wolfe and Rebecca Brenner
TRADE PAPERBACK
978-1-965320-532

10 9 8 7 6 5 4 3 2 1

Look for our titles in paperback, ebook, and audiobook wherever books are sold.
Wholesale offerings for retailers available through Ingram.

ORDERS@WAYFARERBOOKS.ORG
WAYFARERBOOKS.ORG & WAYFARERMAGAZINE.COM

contents

II. Demolish All Three

III. Drafting a Life

Twenty years ago, I lost my mom to opioid addiction.

After her funeral, I inherited a Washington Apples box full of her unpublished poetry, journals, and short stories. Afraid of my anger and grief, I sealed the box and tucked it away.

As a child of addiction, I'd created defenses, strategies, and patterns that centered on orderliness, control, a surface of good and wholesome choices. I once heard a counselor say, "Children of addicts go one of two ways—they develop substance abuse disorder themselves or become control freaks." Nothing would disrupt my meticulously built structure.

Then I became a mother, and all my defenses blew apart. There is no order or control with a newborn. For me to survive—my child and my family, as well—I knew I must face my past. I opened the box.

We are all affected by the opioid crisis. Almost every morning, as I listen to the news after getting my children to school, I hear a story that either directly or indirectly links to the growing crisis. And each morning, my heart aches for the addict and for all of the people who love them.

I am acutely aware that addiction not only affects the addict, it profoundly impacts and shapes the lives of family, friends, co-workers, medical staff, emergency responders—entire communities.

It affects us in distinct ways—loss of lives and relationships, overburdened medical systems, over-crowded courts and prisons, underfunded treatment centers.

However, it also affects us in ways we can't see and are hard to put into words—ways that close down our perspectives, push our nervous systems towards flight-or-fight, and keep us from our own good hearts.

Consciousness is like a house in which the basement is our store consciousness and the living room is our mind consciousness. Mental formations like anger, sorrow, or joy rest in the store consciousness in the form of seeds. We have a seed of anger, despair, discrimination, fear, a seed of mindfulness, compassion, a seed of understanding, and so on. Store consciousness is made of the totality of the seeds, and it is also the soil that preserves and maintains all the seeds. The seeds stay there until we hear, see, read, or think of something that touches a seed and makes us feel the anger, joy, or sorrow. This is a seed coming up and manifesting on the level of mind consciousness, in our living room. Now we no longer call it a seed, but a mental formation.

—THICH NHAT HANH

Seeking but not finding the house builder,
I hurried through the rounds of many births:
Painful is birth ever and again.

O house builder, you have been seen;
You shall not build the house again.
Your rafters have been broken up,
Your ridgepole is demolished too.

—BUDDHA

paper house

Electrical storm

How did she fix her hair the mortician asks he's just finished washing it I'm surprised by my jealousy he gets to touch her still I hand him a picture of Mom the one where she looks like Annie Hall Her favorite I'll die from grief when I see her body but knocked sideways to discover my rage when I see her in the coffin with her gold hawk necklace placed just so on her chest a fiery hot burning blast rattles my body starting warm at my feet it surges through me like an electrical storm sparking wild raging fires in every one of my cells

threatening
to
destroy
every
last
part
of
me

my stepfather Bill is standing behind me I have a vision of wrestling him to the ground, wrapping my small hands around his fat neck and choking him to death instead I run down the hall into a tiny dark room and scream cry slobber until I gain enough composure to go back to her viewing no.

not composure.

more of an old dear friend a mental and emotional structure of viscerally bound tied-tight-for-no-one-ever-to-find suppression of what I know to be right and true after the funeral, when everyone leaves and Bill goes back to work I'm left alone in the North Heide Lane house to sort through Mom's belongings

I
leave
everything
except
for
her
writing

I fill a Washington Apples box with her journals beginnings of sonnets and narratives scratchings on napkins and receipts a small bound unpublished chapbook of her poems I find several of my childhood journals and one of her own on her shelf I grab them too I pack the box away for seven and a half years I'm not brave enough to read any of it

—until I meet you

I.

Survey & Excavate

The city of three rivers.

The skeleton of a new, enormous bridge
out over an endless,
horizon.
Pieces of the earth pulled up,
the mind, bulldozed over.

Navigating through—
a bouquet of dandelions,
held above my head,
to make me taller
and to keep me safe.

Your mother was young—

barely over the shock of you.
A daughter with wounds
stitched over creation.

She fumbled breasts

into your small, searching mouth
unsure what they would give—
her mind a menace.

A tattered cloth heirloom handed down,

tangled threads from her mother,
and her mother before.
She loved you with quaking bones,

hoping you would know.
And you—small and wise—
felt it seep through her skin,

understood the weight of things

before you knew the words for them.
And you drank that love,
terrestrial waters, sweet and bitter both,

embracing the weight of this life,

unable to destroy the world's origins
set deep into your marrow,
silent and true.

Since your birth, I dream myself awake.

Dark in the corner of my room.
Paralyzed,
a loud

SWOOSH out of body.

I expand,

filling my bedroom

then the upstairs

then the house

then the sky.

I am somehow

nowhere and everywhere.

In the middle of the night,

as you nurse,
I am not ready to read my mother's poems, yet.

From my home in Utah,
I walk the perimeters in my mind of Bellevue.

> Right onto Riverview Avenue past the Bellevue sign
> on the Ohio River Boulevard.

> Right onto Meade Avenue—
> an old cobblestone from horse and buggy days.

> Right onto Roosevelt Avenue.
> I know this route like a bridge is burned.

The years silt beneath, I allow myself to stand
on Roosevelt Avenue in front of 532.

This is what it is—a resurrected relative.

I am terrified and exhilarated to be together again.

Drugged

and trapped

in the Roosevelt Avenue basement.

I escape
watch it
explode behind me.

Can see my mom in the distance.

She is uncertain of how this all works.

pacing, restless, her hot breath in my lungs.

A Kodiak bear has awakened

in me since your birth.
She will rip to pieces
anyone who even thinks about harming you.
She trusts no one, not even me—
I could drop you, roll over on you, abandon you.
Her fierceness terrifies me.
In the shower, I catch myself saying,
"I just want to feel like myself again."

But that self is distant,
lost forever, even
haunted by her growl beneath my skin,
pacing, restless, her hot breath in my lungs.
Always there,
lurking behind my eyes,
her claws grazing the inside of my chest.
Even in moments of calm—
your soft breath against my skin,
the quiet weight of your body in my arms—
she prowls, watching, waiting
for the slightest threat.

I miss the woman
who moved freely through the world,
untethered by this wild creature.
Now I walk carefully,
every step measured,
afraid of what might happen
if I loosen my grip,
if I let her out of my sight.

Root of the root

Your dad is back to work, and you and I spend our days sitting on the couch trying to feed and soothe and acquaint—you with me, me with you, me with the root of the root of my heart.

For the first time since her death, I'm desperate to talk to my mom.

I want to know—
What my birth was like?
Did I nurse?
Was she scared?
What kind of baby was I?
Mellow?
Colicky?
I have nowhere to turn but the Washington Apples box.
My entire body trembles.
I open the lid.
I pull the journal out.
My breath catches.

I close my eyes to steady myself and find that I'm walking the perimeters of Bellevue once again.

This time, I start at the Roosevelt Avenue house.
I cannot be here just yet, so I walk.
Up Meade Avenue—past my friend Missy's house, past Heather's house.

I walk past a car parts store, parking lots, old, red brick buildings—until I make it to Lincoln Avenue.

In my mind it's winter, and I can almost feel the cold, damp air chilling my nose. I walk past the bakery, Isly's and a penny candy store.

I turn right onto North Jackson Avenue and arrive at
The Assumption School and Church
      Learning
      Living
      Loving
      Laughing
          Together—
my grade school and church's branding, and I guess mine, too.

I open my eyes and carefully slide Rebecca's First Holy Communion Book out of the box.

Dear Rebecca,

What true happiness! It seems like I've said it over and over, but it's what I really feel. I love you so much and have loved you since before you were even born. I feel like my heart will burst with happiness and pride tonight. Thank you, God, for all you have given us. We are a lucky family!

I hope that the good thoughts that you have today will last a lifetime.

I love you, Rebecca! Mom

Prefaces (Mom)

1961 Tonight I'm back in the old Fairview Dance Hall.
The crystal ball revolves in the ceiling
and sharp fragments of triangular light swirl
around us. Bob Falvo plays the oldies. Scott
English, "High on a Hill," "Chapel of Dreams."

The oldies' low sad tones,
Pied pipers to the hormones.
Musty smells of English Leather,
His varsity jacket
Rubbing rough,
Titillating on my cheek.
Faded Channel #5 on my push-up bra.
Longing, expectation, excitement.
Punctuated by deep base and
high falsetto
swaying, sweating
slow dancing.
Powerful stuff at fifteen.

*

1944 My mother's black and white wedding
picture. Her smile! So expressive, so familiar,
so like my own. She seemed to realize her dreams
in that moment. I would hope that your
chapters were as wonderful as your preface
seemed to be, Mom, except I lived them with you.

The Basement Ritual (Mom)

I'm up through the open-backed cellar steps. Catch a glimpse
of Mom's apron, stretched over her paunchy hips. I am twirled
around by one arm. This is the belt ritual.

I am never sure what I do to start this.

Red-faced Dad holds my one tiny wrist and twists me about in
a sick running dance while my other hand grasps his belt as he
swings it at my legs, tearing bright red stinging welts.

I cry out and jump and whirl around, always waiting for a rescue
from Mom that takes forever to come.

Finally, I hear her voice like some grim torturer saying, "All right,
that's enough now."

I always wondered why I hated Mom more than Dad. Somehow
that passive woman should have helped me. The hatred grew
more intense when I gave birth to my first child.

Some bond between mother and child had been prematurely
broken during those rituals. It left me feeling adrift and distanced
from women most of my adult life.

The stings and welts left on my forming psyche in those years
healed much more slowly than any of the red marks inflicted
upon my skinny legs.

Inside out

I'm in the Roosevelt Avenue basement.
My clothes are in a box.

I write on the wall,
"You have to live from the inside out."
Ink sinking into plaster,
as though the words could remake the cellar.
A window cracked, slow steady air beginning to flow
the walls themselves, exhaling.

Goodnight Becca Beans

Late at night
when the fear threads through the dark
becoming too much for her,
she sneaks into my bed and whispers,
"Come with me Becca Beans."
Pulls away my covers

before I can answer
I go mostly to avoid
my unheated January room.

We sometimes watch shows—
reruns of Star Search, Cheers, The Love Boat.
Sometimes she falls right to sleep
once I slip into the sheets next to her.
Sometimes she has mixed
too many prescription drugs with alcohol

and says the Pittsburgh air makes her sick.
Once we're back in her bed
I tickle her arm as she slips into unconsciousness.

North Freemont Avenue (Mom)

Three room
family rental.

Plastic curtains
and artificial flowers.

Shared bathroom
and thermostat
with other residents.

Smells—
forced air
Christmas tree
baking bread
Irish stew
stale beer
whiskey.

Feelings of innocence
excitement
magic.

Hiding places
from blurry eyes
and sharp fitted breaths—
rough beard.

Feelings of
tinder box conditions
fear
nausea
hiding.

Balph Park (Mom)

Mr. DuMont is his name, I think.
Teaching the little girl to tell time
with a stick drawing in the soft dust.
He sat on the park bench,
she squatted in the dirt by his feet.

A kind, old, patient man.
He wore a derby hat, I think.

At five years of age
she clutched Raggedy Ann books
under her skinny arms.
She climbed an old tree
and perched unnoticed on a garage roof
and read.

She was free and happy here.
No harsh voices.
No bound wrists.
No stinging belts.

Eventually, though, she had to go home.
She was scared then.
Bad things happened.
It sometimes even influences her today,
I know.

Call

the doctor if the baby blues last longer than two weeks,
if you're having trouble sleeping,
if you're having unusual, intrusive thoughts about harming your baby,
if you lose interest in your work, your partner, your life.
That is me.
Nowhere can I find—rest easy, this is a violent upheaval
of every last mental façade that gives a sense of myself,
leaving you instead face to face with a wide-open, pulsating heart,
stripped bare, exposed to a world that feels too sharp,
too loud, each breath trembling with the weight of newness.
That is also me.

Stay with it

I dream I'm stuck
behind a tightly woven mask.

It's tightening,
sending electricity
throughout my body.

It's getting tighter
and tighter
and I compassionately
keep encouraging myself to stay with it.

Stay with it.

The Doll Mother (Mom)

In my dream, I am scattering down those
old, open-backed cellar steps,
jittery fear moving
my feet along quickly,
just ahead of scary,
claw-like hands,
grasping, scratching at my chicken skin
ankles.

Ten baby dolls
propped up in the baby doll crib.
One in the little high chair.
Eleanor and the Raggedies flopped against the wall.
Zippy the monkey on the big bed.
Their little human mother
talked softly and sang to them
covered them with old bath towels
at night
and shared secrets with them in the
dark.

Their friendly fixed eyes witnessed
things
too painful for young dollies to see.
She felt sorry for them
and comforted them
and loved them through it.

She packed them carefully in a box
and put them in the basement
and went away for a while.
She promised she would return
and take them with her
when she was
settled and safe.
Sometimes one must travel light
for survival's sake.

She kept her promise and returned
for them.
They had been thrown away.
Spitefully perhaps, discarded.
Silly to feel such pain
over a box of baby dolls,
especially when you're full grown,
physically.

They were the silent witnesses
those many nights
they knew what their little mother
had to deal with.
They were grateful for her love
while it lasted.

She mislearned some lessons:
to hang on possessively to the
things you love.
To confuse domination and pain
with love and pleasure.
To not trust others.
To feel guilt over self-preservation.

The discovery, the shock—the doll box
is gone.

Dramamine

There is a cobblestone road that leads down away from Roosevelt Avenue to the Ohio River Boulevard.

Mom sends me that way to buy her cigs at the gas station on the corner.

The men always tease me— "How old are you?"

I straighten myself, try to look taller than I am— "I'm ten!"

"Aren't you too young to be smoking?"—they laugh back at me.

I say— "You know they're for my mom."

I toss the money all in coins on the counter and grab the cigs so I can go across the street

to Kentucky Fried Chicken and buy the mini sandwiches—two just for me.

Those men don't understand—I am a kid but I'm not.

Same goes for the pharmacist who always gives me—*me*—a lecture when I buy Dramamine

for Mom.

Like I don't know how stupid these drugs are.

How they make her slur her words and her eyes go all googly in her head.

I call my midwife—

"Is it normal to feel this much anxiety?"

Are you depressed?

"What's the point of life?"

You're depressed.

Too too too tired and disoriented to explain.

It's a blown

        wide

                open

where do we come from where are we going what is this life that
animates me and my baby kind of question?

A bell ringing my chest—

"What is the point of this life?"

Smoking Guns (Mom)

He sat like a stranger with ankle angularly hooked over knee,
rocking, talking about taking what
he would have given me—the house, kids.

Taking?

Talking about sex with her—a numb, slow-motion nightmare.

Why was I being civil?

Still programmed the lady—at all costs.

Beaten and humiliated by a mad man and still poised and
ladylike—*Care for coffee? Show you to the door?*

What he would give me?

What about what I had given him?

Given God?

Committed freely, turned over my whole life?

All my dreams, my hopes, my soul to him and now, alone
unattached, I find that that was "unhealthy" to do—codependent.

I'm confused about being a wife, a woman, a Christian.

I go for her

I watch her when she dances in the dining room late at night.
I'm used to her waking me for our nightly rendezvous ever since
my dad left so I anticipate her arrival.

My mother of the night is more emotional more spacey more
talkative than my mother of the day.

The nights she doesn't come I worry she is too sick or too sad or
dead.

So I go for her.

When I can't find her in her bed I become anxious and begin my
journey through the cold
dark house in hopes of finding her together alive.

I find her most nights
swaying
crying
to seemingly no music at all—
one hand holds her beer the other sways to the music only she
can hear through the head phones.

Her eyes are closed and her face is drenched with tears.

She has on one of my dad's old white undershirts and blue and
pink flowered underpants
two sizes too big for her. I think how small how alive her naked
arms and legs look in comparison to the oversized dark brown
hutch that houses the stereo.

To be so alive seems scary
overwhelming
disorienting.

I sit on the far corner of the living room couch
in the dark
watching her.

And I stay here
hardly breathing
until she climbs the stairs to find her bed.

Too much (Mom)

I talked with my new counselor about the basement on North
Freemont Avenue—the abuse issues.

I feel scared once again.

Perhaps so much of me is based on having slightly flawed but
good parents that if that memory
were to return and reveal things of a dark nature, the anger, rage
and disconnectedness would be too much.

A marriage

that doesn't hold the same shape forever
isn't a failure—
this illumination is not an accident.
A ring taken off is a
soft, yet definite clearness of
air where something solid used to be,
gentle space redefining its edges.

Between us now—
bodies that never conceptualize themselves,
we allow what is—
atoms placed randomly then further apart,
orbiting in their quiet pull,
moving, not lost.
Together or alone, I'm told,
we can still close our eyes and see God.

II.

Demolish All Three

Pittsburgh

I dream my husband, a man and I are walking down a street.

The man asks why I haven't been to Pittsburgh in five years.

I lie
and say
I'm not sure.

He asks how my mom feels about that.

I choke back tears and say, *She died.*

I'm suddenly ashamed, embarrassed, and sorry my partner must
hear all this again.

I feel moved
to lie down on the city sidewalk.

I somehow know
that Pittsburgh
and the earth
want to absorb the pain
of losing
my
mom.

I'm startled awake by the
buzzing tenderness emanating
from my chest.
My sweat has soaked through
my clothes
and my sheets.

I lie still,
breathe deep,
and tell myself it's ok
to feel this.

Stay with it.

There is something comforting,
reassuring,
in this bit of tenderness.

Elton John

Bill says she walked up to him at an AA meeting, he introduced himself and she said, "I'm not interested." Thought, *What an arrogant woman.* Her second-hand clothes and botched Bowie hair were a turn off. He says, "Three days later, I couldn't stop thinking of her." Mom says she doesn't remember.

> I watch her get ready—
> a pair of jeans
> white t-shirt
> and pink jean jacket
> Maybelline mascara
> Tickle deodorant
> Aquanet hairspray..

Bill says he hates Elton John, but when my mom tapped the beat of *Tiny Dancer* on his thigh he knew he was in love.

> I sit with Katie—
> under a blanket
> on cement city stairs
> on Roosevelt Avenue
> and wait.

They pull up in Bill's big blue Cadillac and we can't see in the window because it's late.

Mom makes us go inside, tells us to go to bed, but I'm anxious to hear all about her date

with the doctor.

Between fantasy and reality (Mom)

I'm having trouble, thinking on this matter of forgiving Dad.

Being an only child and the only girl, it seems it's important for me to have a dad to look up to and to be proud of—like the handsome heroes in the movies. It's also clear to me that Our Father says to forgive others if we are to be forgiven.

But somewhere between the fantasy and the reality of Dad, the truth gets lost. Some of it lost forever I hope, to be truthful.

Dad's nasty, mean name-calling and hurtful hitting and beating with the belt wasn't so good. I have memories, really vague, like having my hands tied behind my back and lying on Dad's bed.

What I really remember of that day is Mom coming home and them having a really bad fight. I remember this fight. I know for absolute certain that Mom won, because it never happened again.

Forget everyone and everything

I call Dad— *Was Mom abused by Grandpap?*

He tells me a story I've never heard.

Just past his parents' house on Riverview Avenue is an old
cobblestone road that leads down to the train tracks.

When he and Mom were in high school, there used to be a train
station there.

He found her there one afternoon—planning to run away, she
said, no more belts no more bound wrists.

Bound wrists.

I tell him I have found that several times in her writing.

Suddenly, so much about my mom makes sense—and in the
space of clarity, a compassion for the little girl she was awakens.

Vast

I am in a

                                        vast,

clear ocean—

                    the world dissolved by waves.

I'm fighting off an old man
who is trying to pull me
deep
down
into
the
water.

I reluctantly tell the baby
floating on an old tree,
to jump to me.

She jumps with no fear
all joy and trust into my arms—
the beginning of a huge adventure.

The man gives one last violent yank.

I struggle to keep us afloat.

Call me what I am the watery folds of cortex—

weaving through skull, shaping neurons, dendrites and axons into clear pathways of hypervigilance.

Call me what I am a body that grew so complex throughout evolutionary history that it had to create a nervous system and brain—a type of command center—No. I'm not a brain that has life but rather life that created a brain.

Call me what I am an electro-chemical reaction—searching through the possibilities of all matter. Folding in the information gathered from experience throughout the timeline of existence, encoded on each amygdala. No. No.

Call me what I am a river running who keeps trying to dam her own shores.
All pulse and flow and push this life a beneficiary of all who came before.

Call me what I am the phenomena world.
Vigilance a solid grey rock, life slips around, even under.

Call me what I am particles and atoms of the first galaxies and stars.
Lineage an energy signature reminding me to act my age.

Call me what I am the world my body.
Love eddies, then floods the shrine of cells bundled tight against
the lungs.

Call me what I am a mystery.
A never-ending surrendering where I enter again and again.

The exam (Mom)

I quiet myself, God. More methodically, more expertly, more probing—with my own introspective fingers. I begin to examine. I gingerly feel along—exploring under my rib cage, into secret places. Feeling for little bumps, little tumors of instinctive fears, reservations, beginning malignancies of skepticism, doubt— fingers creep along, looking for those deep deep roots of caution. Stop—go another direction. I sense how important this exam is—if I miss something—. You see, these instincts of mine have kept me alive. I've been sober for six months. God help me. I've searched carefully.

Cleaning the basement

We are moving
to North Heide Lane
and Mom says
it's time to clean out the basement.

She has friends
from AA come help us move.

A neighbor
has to use a potato
cut in half
to get a broken light bulb
out of two sockets—
one above the washing machine
and one above the urine-soaked rugs.

I can tell Mom is embarrassed—
there are piles of dog shit everywhere
so she makes me help her carry
the soggy piss rug
up the cellar stairs
through the house
down the wooden stairs
to the city stairs
to the curb.

I step over the thin, icy puddles
that melt with the slightest warmth
from the thread on my shoes
because my socks
shorts
and shirt
are already soaked through with dog urine.

I don't want to be here.
I hate this house
this street
this city—
nothing good happens here anymore.

Mom assures me
that North Heide Lane will be better—
with the walk-in closets
and the in-ground pool
with the water slide.

The boys are moving into their own apartment.
They don't want to move in with Bill.

She says the doctor will take care of us.

I'm not so certain.

The counselor talks about decisions

—choices—cause and effect.

You have made very different choices than your mother.
Your choices will have a different outcome.
Your path and life are not hers, they are yours.

I'm holding the phone to my ear, shaking my head yes.

We all learn how to see, to think from our parents and families.

My eyes swell tears.

The catch is we don't learn that we're learning, so how things are
presented when we're young, we take to be just how things are. And those
teaching us, most times don't know what they are really teaching us.

I am still shaking my head, trying to believe it.

But, your mother's life didn't just happen. She had her own unhealed
trauma and no support or tools to help her navigate. You are here. You
are learning for both of you.

I close my eyes, still gripping the phone, the ground pulsing
beneath me.

Two little girls (Mom)

She stands straight,
chin regally lifted in the spotlight.

Her young body blooming bashful.

Awkwardly, alternately constricted
and revealed by leotards and chiffon.

A smashed down breast,
a near naked buttock—
sexual and disorienting for a parent.

The Chariots of Fire theme song plays
and she dances,
not watching the teacher as her peers do.
She breaks loose from the pack
leaps
glides
jumps
across the stage.

A strangely quiet audience
uncomfortable with her intensity.

I sit watching this child.

Mine.

I remember myself at eleven.
Frightened and gangly.

I hid.

Trembling in closets among big shoes,
crouched in deep window wells with crunchy leaves,
waiting for the verbal storms to pass.

I curled into a tight little ball
in a velvet-topped window seat,
hiding from my would-be nurturer.

The spotlight was my enemy.

In the audience,
tears of pride for my bowing ballerina;
tears of sadness still creep in
for the cowering little girl who was.

Obvious route

I'm in a small, room

just off the basement.

It's narrow.

People are sitting at tables

right up against the walls.

At first I focus on the room,

the people, the tables.

Then I switch my attention to what's outside—

an ocean raging against the wall.

How flimsy and breakable is the silly wall.

I'm now walking along the shore,

with the people from the narrow room.

The ocean comes up and pulls me in a bit

and then a huge wave surges, pulling and pushing

us everywhere.

I find a path between the ocean and the shore.

It seems like such an obvious route.

Intrusive thoughts

The counselor is teaching me about intrusive thoughts.
Thoughts I don't want—but that keep coming, looping visceral in
my body.
Thoughts are just thoughts.
Thoughts are just thoughts.
Thoughts are.
There is more than just my thinking.
Let's go back.
I want to tell my mom this—that she wasn't broken.
Tell her there is a way.
Let's start with how attention keeps flying open—in my dreams
and in my waking life.
An intrusive thought and then swoosh!
Attention lands right where there is space and openness,
potential, light—electric.
Free. Like a game of Chutes and Ladders—
I land back in my body, alive, awake and raw.
Is this an awakening or am I losing it, just like my mother?
I remember she didn't go crazy.
She had her own cause and effect—she didn't have support. And
maybe I can start to trust what I'm feeling.
I tell the counselor I feel like I'm losing my mind.
He laughs. Says, "You are."
I laugh too, because what I'm losing is my unconscious fusion
with every thought that comes through.

Let's go back.

Intrusive thinking is a training ground.

The more absurd, the easier to see they are just thoughts, most
days.

Let's start with where I was fused and identified, where self was
once home

is   nothing   and

                                    no   one

— just potential.

Our starting point

The midwife tells me to walk—it will help to soothe postpartum.

I do—but it's 100 degrees outside and you cry the entire time and my body just wants to rest, be still, be soothed, and cared for.

It's all so new yet very familiar—feeling like running, but really needing rest.

That first day of High School—laying out the black and white checked skirt Bill bought for me. My heart was pounding hard, trying to break out into my throat. I wanted to cry, but I practiced smiling in the mirror instead.

In that new outfit and new town, no one knew my mom was an alcoholic. I became an expert in how to fit in, to move, to go. No one would find what I was running from, even me.

It's 5 am and it's already hot, I have a screaming baby—this, this is now.

This is what we have to work with, B—this is our starting point.

Let them fall off

I'm in the basement again.

The far back wall is covered in windows and doors.

They are broken—barely hanging on to their hinges.

I keep trying to put them back on.

Mom is here, encouraging me to let them all fall off.

This Gets His Attention (Mom)

We had a big fight—
I behaved badly—door slamming—irrational screaming.

I'm sure I scared Bill, and probably gave him pause about me—
revealed that insane side.

My looming fears.
Big ugly fuckers!

"I am crazy, out of control, unlovable, deserve to be dumped.
After all, isn't that why Gary dumped me—

I am so impossible
I lose my self-worth so very easily.
My stomach swells up for three days.

This gets attention from Bill—
I perversely love this.

Your hand on my face.

Me leaning in, allowing life to continue.

Each touch an act on life's behalf.
We can't help it, we're shrines to our ancestors,

a journey we all make together, this
becoming the world. With you, I've forgotten the

way to think, to speak, as life floods through, washes
its body, cares for the children, writes a poem, continues.

Look, is that shadow us? The answer—much larger
than the question in my thoughts, now a tangled,

thicket. I name them—brown eyes in sunlight, black lashes
blinking. Vigilance its own weight. My allegiance to my

aliveness, now. A life pierced by yours, the wound the entrance.
Nothing left but a motiveless passion for life.

I didn't expect this to be a part of becoming a mother.

Not anymore

I can see the Roosevelt Avenue basement again and it's clean and sorted.

> I am somewhere else.
> A new place I can't quite
> make sense of yet.
> I'm simply amazed.

> It's bright and spacious.

I can sense the small windows above the washing machine are blowing open.

I can see the kitchen.

The back door won't stay closed or locked.

Someone has cleared out all of the old stacked up boxes and bags of garbage from the back room.

I startle awake.

There's a palpable tenderness radiating from my chest.

My mind shakes like a dog kicking off water.

You cracked the moment open like a nut—

stated, "The stars are ghosts." Stood outside
of the screen door, barely an outline,
a shadow between the porch light and the dark.
I asked if dying was hard. "Yes," you said, "at first."
I wanted to know more,

but you told me to stop—

the night, holding its breath,   glorious,

expansive,

and silent.

I asked, "What is the meaning of life?"
and you told me with a voice like insects,   "To delight."
Then,

emptiness with a deep darkness came through the back door.

Emptiness

As I look into my spinning thoughts, I find an emptiness.

The emptiness spills over into other mental structures—how a birth should be, how nursing should go, how a baby should be, how a mother should act, and what a family should be.

It's all crumbling.

They are all stories.

No human power (Mom)

Come to me now, my lord, as a shy lover.
One who waits vulnerably outside the door
until all others have gone.
Come tenderly in to me now.
Let me feel your warm arms around me.
Ease my fears, my loneliness, my longings.

My husband distances from me and becomes cold.
His features harden and I feel the trap being baited
with the absence of love.

I become frightened and childlike,
cowering, fighting back tears,
feeling the old familiar chest pain.

I sit at the table eating, tasting nothing,
as the waiter solicitously passes by.
All joy, past, present, and future, erased from my life.
No conversation—
I should be grateful for the silence.

Words and sentences finally come from him.
He admits to dichotomies I already sense.
Part of him longs for his freedom,
his solitude,

his independence,
unencumbered.

Is he laying the groundwork for an exit statement?
Where do I go with my pent up passion this
Saturday evening?
To dance, to feel the music, to make love?
To be fulfilled in a way I've never experienced?

I do as I've been taught and ask God for help.
I try acceptance.
I count my blessings.
I swallow my tears.
I share and give support to others in AA.
Where and when will my help come?

I run inside myself staying inconspicuous in my pain.
He picks away at his food and at me
as I try to eat,
trapped in my silence.

At home, I invite him to sit with me a moment.
Stay with me awhile, my love.
Let me smell your sweet aroma,
feel your strong arms,

your grasping hands.
Hold me for even a short time
and tell me you love me.
Show me in a simple way I will understand.

These pleasures don't seem meant for me.
Perhaps if I were different:
more intelligent
much sexier
a little thinner.
Then he would be interested in me!
I know this is a futile line of reasoning.

He has always taken care of me
like a needy, bungling child;
and I allow it, welcome it.
I nobly, naively search for my God;
I seek out the good in people,
actions that have no practical value to him,
and he quickly bores with my musing.

Oh God, I need to feel my mate's love tonight.
I know that will not happen.

Come to me now, my Lord, as a shy lover.
One who waits vulnerably outside the door
until all others have gone.
Come tenderly in to me now,
let me feel your warm arms round me.
Ease my fears, my loneliness, my longings.
I believe that you can do all things.
Please touch me tonight.

III.

Drafting A Life

Warm and wet, it dances you

vibrating through your cells,
up through your veins and nerve endings,
orchestrating the rhythm of your heart and lungs.

Nobody owns it—yet it's everywhere.

These mountains.

This sky—this wide deep blue sky
with the grey storm clouds building over rounded hills.

Any story I try to tell you about this aliveness

is not at all like yourself feeling it
buzzing and humming through your bones.

How it flushes your skin warm and pink

or draws the hairs on your neck up,
making you shiver.

We can't pin any part of it down,

our bodies intimate
with life unfolding.
It's a mystery,

Let's surrender and enter our bodies once again.

The Doll Mother Part II (Mom)

Bill awakens me.

I am crying
hard, which is uncharacteristic of me.

It has probably been twenty years since I
have thought of those dolls.

I crawl closer to Bill
and cry some more and tell him the dream.

He already knows much about the old North Freemont house
and
that basement with its smells of leather and
alcohol.

Nice to not keep secrets.

Shortly after that night,
we are getting in the car one evening to go to dinner
and I open my
door to find Raggedy Ann and Andy sitting in
my seat, smiling,
waiting for me.

#

Talked softly to,
sung to
in the night.
Cradled gently in protective arms.
Given the freedom to find my way
and exorcise my demons.

I am just understanding that
trust and love are neat!

Not to be hoarded!

He is a remarkable husband.

A professional man no less!

(No less is probably necessary)

He doesn't hurt me.

The dolls would be happy.

They say, nap when the baby naps.

I do, most days.

And each afternoon I wake up with a raw heart.

Painful, really.

Scared awake by a

boundless

throbbing

Like an old wound, pushed and picked into.

I have to encourage myself to stay with it.

Before, I would have rushed out of bed knee deep in my list of things to do.

But now—

in this nowhere land of postpartum days nowhere to run nowhere to go I let myself stay with it—

the rawness,

the tenderness

the vulnerability.

I know, I know (Mom)

I need a nap.

Perhaps with rest will come some relief from my belly swelling.

I do look forward to some feedback or intimacy from my mate—I know, I know—don't make it happen. I'm withering a bit.

Just let my search and reliance be on you, God—I really don't need the pain.

I'm tiring myself out with this.

This is definitely not Fred Astaire (Mom)

If He were to hold me in His arms
and we would dance and glide
among the packed sand,
He would throw His head back
and laugh
as I tried to follow His steps.

I would laugh too!
We are an odd couple,
He so tall and me so small.
But I hold onto Him with faith, trust
and love.

Sometimes we join seagulls in flight;
we just glide upwards with them.
A natural extension of our dance.

He shows me city tenements;
I see men sniffing cocaine in back alleys.
People frantic with purposeless activity.
I see families around Formica
topped dinner tables.
Peaceful and laughing and loving
one another.

I ask Him, "What's the difference?
Why some peaceful?
Why some frantic?"
He laughs as He holds my hands
through the soft updraft.
"Some never take time to dance with Me."

I don't ask a lot of questions

Part because I'm a kid and I don't know life or the moment to be
any different than how it is right now.

And part because I've learned to be quiet, to listen, to learn
through what gets revealed—
somehow this approach feels smarter, safer.

So, when we move into Bill's house, I just notice.

I notice how big and clean and new the North Heide house is.

The white carpets vacuumed into perfect triangles.

The sparkling, oversized kitchen appliances.

The clean windows in the living room that look out onto a deck
that overlooks an in-ground pool
with a diving board and a water slide.

I notice how there are two two-car garages—one is reserved
solely as Bill's work room.

I notice how "my room" has three closets—one walk-in that is
bigger than my bedroom on Roosevelt Avenue—and an attached
bathroom with two sinks and a mirror that takes up an entire wall.

I also notice how there is barely any furniture.

Out of the fourteen rooms in the house, only four are furnished and even light fixtures and lamps are scarce.

My mom sees me watching.
She tells me that Bill's soon to be ex-wife, cheated on him.

That Bill found pictures of her and her boyfriend in the glove compartment of her car.

That when Bill was at work, she came and emptied out his house, even taking the chandelier
that hung over the dining room table.

That they are in a bitter divorce battle and Bill is paying through the teeth on alimony, lawyer fees and court cost.

She says it will be over soon, though.

Satellite (Mom)

When Gary left—I guess he symbolized so many things that were kind, sincere, loving, and gentle. If a basically good person like Gary found me so destructive and unbearable, what good was I? I wonder if I'll ever really recover my sense of being a good person?

It's so strange changing partners at this time in my life. I sometimes feel a bittersweet longing for the old songs and carefree old partner, but I'm sure I confuse this longing for that of youth gone by. Bill has such an uncanny sense in knowing what's right for me.

I don't have a clue what's right for Bill—God seems to take care of that. Strange—God takes care of Bill, Bill takes care of me. Who do I take care of?

This is a story (Mom)

This is a story about Bill.

This is a story about his fatigue—
his mental anguish.

A story about Bill's struggle with a concept
of a loving God.

A story about Bill's restrained, reigned in
emotions.

A story about Bill's emotions always
kept on a tight leash.

This is a story about the storyteller
and the listener who loves him.

Whirling Dervishes

You continue to cry—all the time. Each night for three months, I shush and suckle and sway you—all day and most of each night. Yet, I can't soothe you and neither of us sleep. Tonight— shushing, suckling, and swaying in your nursery, worn down to my bones, not able to go on a moment longer—I have a vision. Generations of women from every nationality shushing, suckling and swaying with us. A community of whirling mother dervishes giving me the strength to get you to sleep and to try it all again tomorrow. It feels ceremonious, like I am being given my place in an endless lineage of mothers. I remember a call and response song Mom and I use to sing:

Becca, come out and play with me
and bring your dollies three,
climb up my apple tree.
Slide down my rain slide,
into my cellar door
and we'll be jolly friends
for evermore.

Mommy, I can't come play with you
my dollies have the flu,
boo-hooy-hooy-hoo.
I have no rain slide,
I have no cellar door
but we'll be jolly friends
for evermore.

I bow my head to see you've finally fallen asleep.

Making you smile (Mom)

I hope this annulment is for the right reasons, God. I believe
it is—although I hope I don't get my expectations too high
concerning Billy and Holy Communion— just help me stay
focused on me.

I wonder if everyone has the natural capacity to reach out, soul to
soul, at gut level, and experience the pain, joy, feelings of another
human being? Is it always a battle between logic and feeling? I
wonder. Intellect and reason vs. intuition and love? I wonder
if it separates order from chaos? It provides a sort of structure,
I guess. After all, look what happened to the love, peace and
brotherhood of the hippies? The musings are fun—maybe some
of us (moi)—it's not that we are helpless or lazy—but maybe our
function is to "muse"—to observe and record—maybe if I have
the gift of feeling what other people feel and believing that we
all, on a very fundamental level, have the very same desires and
pains and joys and questioning—maybe if I have that gift of heart
or empathy and that belief—it is my talent to record it—to make
that bridge for people—make people laugh—not feel so different
or isolated. What's my gift God that you really want me to make
use of, as in making you smile?

Abandon hope

I read these words—abandon hope—in a Buddhist book, and they land in a way that changes everything.

Before you were born, I used to think hope was everything.

We had so much hope when Mom first got sober.

So much hope when we moved from Roosevelt to North Heide.

So much hope—always.

A compliment

Bill says
that a kid like me—
who's been through what I've been through—
shouldn't always be smiling
and so happy.

He says
I'm
"off."

But I take this
as a compliment.

My smiles
are my defense.

I'm not letting anyone in—
even myself.

Sane thinking (Mom)

God, could you please remove this sick, twisted, false belief I have about the euphoria I can find in drugs?

Please restore me to sane thinking as you have with alcohol and cigarettes.

Relapse Prevention (Mom)

1. Don't get overly tired
2. Don't get overly hungry
3. Stay out of denial
4. Watch for resentment
5. Face and handle self-pity
6. Impatience with sobriety
7. Impatience with NA
8. Watch frustrations
9. Watch cockiness
10. Complacency
11. Keep up with depression (Frozen anger and self-pity)
12. No internal criticisms of others
13. Try not to distrust the motives of others
14. Stay away from slippery people and places
15. Follow directions
16. Avoid argumentative state
17. Avoid "withdrawal or isolation"
18. Don't switch addictions
19. Do not refuse to go to NA
20. Get a home group, meetings, steps
21. Get a sponsor
22. Have gratitude
23. Prayer and recognize answers

I pray for those still using and in relapse.

I pray

I pray for all those still using and in relapse.

I pray for all the people who love them.

Sane, but bombarded

I dream I'm in the Roosevelt Avenue basement.

It's been turned into a hospital.

All I hear are non-stop announcements of how patients are going crazy—one after another.

A voice says, "Someday this is going to be you."

I'm swimming,
dripping
in confusion.

I feel "on" so I don't lose it.

I'm sane
but bombarded,
teetering on some unseen edge.

Rushing

The slow pace of postpartum is revealing a part of myself that is constantly rushing.

Rushing while I eat.

Rushing while I shower.

Rushing while I drive.

Rushing from one moment always into the next and the next and the next.

I can feel the Rusher in my clenched jaw, gripped shoulders and shallow breath.

A physical manifestation of a mental habit—a way of being— surviving.

With my hand on my heart, I ask, "Why are you rushing?"

I hear, "Must keep going to prove that life is worth living"—the collective cry of children raised in addiction.

A desperate yowl from my heart—*life is good, worth living, right?*

The counselor says, "Bill may not have been good for your mother, but he was certainly good for you.'"

He is right.

I was fourteen when we first moved in with Bill from the north side of Pittsburgh. I had one small bag of a few pieces of clothing, a purple stuffed rabbit named Honey Bunny and several journals. The home we were leaving was over 100 years old and falling down. The wooden stairs and front porch had huge holes that you had to slowly walk around, not causing the rest of the stairs and porch to collapse.

Bill's home was ten years old.

It had white carpets in every room, vacuumed into perfectly formed triangular shapes. The bedroom that was to be mine had three closets.

His house also had an in-ground pool with a water slide and diving board. This is where I spent the majority of the first summer that we lived with him.

Just the change in zip codes was enough to change my life— the school, the resources—opened up an entire world of opportunities that were not available to me days before. I was aware of this. I knew that my future could, would look very different from the South Hills—and I wanted it.

We had only been there a few weeks—I was sitting at the pool and he walked down to ask if he could take me shopping. Said he knew how the kids dressed in the South Hills and he could help me.

I accepted.

I was about to enter the 9th grade in a school and town I had never lived. And here was this gracious offer—to help ease the transition.

During our family dinners—which we never ate on a regular basis before—Bill would give etiquette lessons. What fork was for what and when it was to be used. Where the butter went, where your napkin went, how to chew. All information no one had taught me and I was eager to learn.

He even taught me how to answer the phone. When I would pick up and say, "This is her." he yelled from his den, "This is she!"

He taught me how to drive.

Came to every one of my dance and theater performances.

Made sure I took my SAT's.

Took me to look at colleges.

And   yet, he and Mom were enmeshed in the fraught exchange of trust and pills, their bond both clinical and complex. He carried his own unattended trauma, radiating silently from every cell.

I can't escape this dichotomy.

I can't keep running from it.

I won't make it to the other side unless I go through.

NA Worksheet (Mom)

Name a person in the family that has been affected by your drug use:
Rebecca (daughter)

List how/what/when they have been affected and be specific:
How:
Her extreme worry and anxiety concerning her mom and "best friend"

What:
My drug abuse and hospital stays (she began to catch on)

When:
Her whole life, but mostly the last two years

List specific things/ways/communication/interactions you will do to make a sober difference in the way you interact with this person:
Walk the walk

Listen to your gut

Mom calls me
from her hospital room
at Washington Hospital.
I am standing in
my apartment
on Bainbridge Island.

Listen to your gut
I tell her to listen to her gut,
as if it's that simple, as if
the body's whispers aren't drowned by the weight of others'
wants.
I stand, miles away,
my feet planted on the hardwood floor,
steady—yet knowing I'm asking her to push against a tide
she's lived in for years.
Listen to your gut.
I don't say how much courage it takes
to hear yourself over the noise.
How many times have we both been talked out of our own
knowing,
told we were too afraid, too weak, too wrong?
But in this moment, I need her to believe
that the flutter of doubt she feels
is not a failure,

but a guide.
In the pause between her breath and mine,
I hear it—
the slow gathering of her strength,
the pushback she's been waiting to give
all her life.
For now, in this quiet space,
she agrees—
and I feel proud,
but also afraid,
because I know how quickly the voices return
like the tide,
pulling her back to shore.

From hospital bed with acute angina (Mom)

The three garbage bags sit—
I once again feel sadness—
childlike desire that I'm leaving
the old gracious homes of my childhood dolls and books—
the wonderful places I retreated to—
not the three-bedroom apartment
and basement
on North Freemont—
such sadness—
a strong desire to be a child in a story.

Busted

I can't get into the Roosevelt Avenue house—the bottom cement city stairs have dissolved into the earth.

The top wooden stairs that led to the house are all busted to pieces.

Bill calls in the early morning,

asks what time it is in Seattle.

I grab my glasses,
look at the clock,
and say 6:43 a.m.

He says, "Your mother has died."

I take
a cab
to a ferry
to a cab
to a plane
to make it back to Pittsburgh,
back to North Heide Lane.

I have a vision.

Mom and I are surrounding a young girl to show her support and love.

She asks, "Is life pointless?"

I answer, "I don't know."

"If it is, can this realization be freeing instead of nihilistic?" she asks.

I say, "I'm not sure."

Lit from within

You and I are in and out of sleep all morning on the couch.

I have a vision of hundreds of women from my family's past, generation upon generation walking up from behind me and each ceremoniously taking a small piece of the crown on my head— their story, fear, worry.

Each time a piece is removed, a bit of bright white light shines out from within me.

By the end, the crown of my head is vibrating so intensely it goes clear, and light shines unencumbered from within.

I see thousands of women behind me and thousands of women ahead of me and we are all connected through our hearts—a line of light going back and ahead as far as I can imagine.

I awaken to the now familiar grinding-up heart.

Do I have the courage to live into what is unfolding?

The rainbow

Riding on the ferry
to the cab
to the airport
I think,
"She'll never get to see the Northwest
or Ireland
or the ocean again."

Perfectly timed,
the clouds part
and a dense, vibrating
rainbow arches through
the opening to the surface of the ocean.

I think,
"This is bullshit!
I don't want a rainbow
a metaphor
a poem;
I want my mom
sober
healthy
and alive!"

I turn away from the window—
the rainbow
the metaphors
the hope—
and I feel the anger
close in on me
like the low clouds
almost covering the ocean
from view.

I let myself condense
and close.

I never want to open again—
not to this world
not to this life
not to these moments.

True courage

In and out of sleep all night long while you sleep snuggled between your dad and me.

Quiet and still in our bedroom. All that's here in these late-night moments are mind and heart.

Pay attention to how mind keeps scrambling, trying to build up structures.

Sink and bob in the sensations of the broken-down structures create through body—the carefully crafted mind is at once secure and claustrophobic, letting it all crumble.

Lay here, reminded that the only real choice is to open and let it all fall down. Again and again and again. And in time, maybe it will become less frequent—new structures will fill up the spaces. And maybe we'll even get more comfortable in the spaces themselves.

Electrical storm

"How did she fix her hair?" the mortician asks.

He's just finished washing it.

I'm surprised by my jealousy—he gets to touch her, still.

I hand him a picture of my Mom—the one where she looks like Annie Hall.

Her favorite.

I think—I'll die from grief when I see her body.

I don't.

I rage and scream and cry and slobber.

But I don't die.

The thing about funerals is they are the worst and best moments of your life.

—If you're lucky, your grief is met with an outpouring, overflowing, river of love that carries you.

—Like my brothers waiting for me at the Pittsburgh International Airport.

—Or my friend—Stephanie, who could see I just wanted to be in bed instead of downstairs being polite at my mother's wake and gathered all my friends to leave so my family wouldn't force me to socialize.

—Or my friend—Adrienne, who brought me bags of vegan and vegetarian food so I'd have healthy food to eat.

—Or when I had been in bed too long and my childhood friend Justin let himself in, made me tea and breakfast and forced me out of bed into the kitchen out the door and for a hike every day for almost a month.

These moments, gestures, friends are the steps walking me through.

The note

On the last day of Mom's viewing I tuck a note next to her hand in the coffin.

I'm sorry Mom.

I wish I'd known how to help you.

I wish I'd stayed closer.

I wish I'd known what to do.

I love you.

miracle eyes blinking,

the entire veil lifted.

Small circling lips, hands clenched in tiny fists—
all perspectives burst away.

The ways I had to protect myself
from sour breath, incoherent words,

I, too, was once fresh like you—
a miracle, life simply expressing itself.

    At first, I wanted the awakening to stop—
for the clear seeing to cloud,

to be just like the other moms,
clipping small bows and pressing tan pants.

    But my wanting meant nothing to life,
        shining brilliant from your eyes.

I cried with you on my chest,
telling you I probably wasn't the best choice.

You pulled the corner of your mouth up—
maybe a smile, a small hiccup—then threw up milk on my shirt.

    I knew then I'd at least try to love my terror,
        to find my own shining brilliance again.

She asks me if I hated her,

as a mom.

We're in the Roosevelt Ave. basement.

I hug her, now on the city stairs.

I say, I'm angry.

That my anger is like an old run-down structure that I keep
finding myself caught in.

I tell her I know that structure has been
cleaned
cleared
opened
remolded and knocked down—at times.

I assure her that I am certain, beyond the confines of my anger is
a deep, nourishing current, a welcoming abyss an endless ocean.

I tell her I know it's there that my love for her is—where my
heart is free.
I'm just not sure yet how to not get caught.

But I will stay with it. I promise her I promise myself.

Seeing

Allan and I are at a wedding and you are at home with a babysitter.

Tonight, it's early evening on a ranch in Park City and the summer light is pouring through the Aspen trees, lighting up the tiny buckles on my sandals.

This is the most lasting change that has stayed with me since the day you were born—this ability to see, to notice.

I can now see the subtle yet distinct differences in the hues of each hollyhock that lines the yard.

Or how one type of wild grass seems to sway right to left in the wind while another moves in circles.

Or how immaculately and precisely this doctor and his wife who sit across from us are dressed.

He's talking about how much trouble Joan Rivers' doctors are in—what a devastating mistake they made.

He goes on—his own brother almost died in the hands of a misinformed nurse.

I mention how my mom died in a hospital.

"How? She must have been so young?"—familiar questions.

I tell him the story Bill told me—it was early morning, my mom was having trouble breathing, the nurse came in and gave her oxygen, she was better, the nurse stepped out for a moment and when she returned Mom was gone.

I mention how I always wondered if she was accidentally overdosed.

The immaculate doctor says, "Yes—those are the symptoms of someone overdosing."

Allan excuses himself for whiskey.

I go to the bathroom.

I lock myself in and breath deep down into my toes.

The truth of it lands in my body.

I don't cry. In the bathroom at the wedding or on the ride home.

I don't cry until the babysitter asks how my evening was and I don't know what to say.

I sit on the deck with Allan and go through it all one more time with him.

Allan has become skilled at listening, just listening.

Our actions matter. Our choices matter.

Mom's poems and your sweet smile, and now Emerson's, have helped me see this.

I've become certain that my own heart is something I can live into.

Its voice lives in the space of the quiet.

If I pay attention, it speaks to me through lady bugs landing on my thigh, wet, slobbery toddler kisses, bright hollyhocks and my dreams each night.

Address

the landscape directly—
Rough-fruited fairybells
Chicories, then endives
Showy Goldeneye dusting golden hips.
Make offerings

to the dead who keep changing.
Taste their lineage on a pricked finger.
A direct script from a life already
gone blue to red.
Become the world

fan fingers out through the grasses—
Lungs mirroring the lightning,
braiding into the bronchi what they know—
the earth is a giant electrical circuit
us, its weak conductors.

There is no private salvation.
The winds may worsen. Confusion total—
but there are shapes,
structures knit close to the bones to ease the flow.
Bring the ritual to a close

attending to all that's left.
Life carries its own body,
washes its skin once home.
Cares for the children, continuing.
Lay down
intimacy is slow,
but our reverence can be deep.

Experiencing Rebecca (Mom)

The older I become, the more I grow up in sobriety and
experience, the deeper understanding
and insight I have of my mother—the more I am filled with guilt,
laughter, respect and tears for opportunities that I lost with her.

I wonder if death and absence has glamorized or exaggerated my
feelings about her—somehow, I don't think so.

1886–1994—
Catherine,
Isabelle,
Patricia,
Rebecca,
Katie—
one hundred and ten years of Irish women.

An old black and white photo of a white-haired smiling lady in
a wheelchair—very dim memories of riding on Grandmother
Catherine's wheelchair in the convalescent home.

Confusion concerning the tales passed down to me by my
mother—was it the gas running on the stove or her head in the
oven?

My mother bared stories of her childhood and her own mom.

I will always want to know more.

I listened to those who told me I should write—it's like those people who tell you your whole life you're not "living up to your real potential." What is potential anyhow?

And furthermore, what's real potential? Is there unreal potential or fantasy potential? Or can I live down to it?

So—what should I write? To whom? Why should I? Where do I begin? And how high is up?

Because I am a people pleaser at heart, I will try to share some of my experiences with you before and after my awakening at 42.

Some have made me laugh; some have made me cry.

Some filled me with joy and good self-worth; some cut me off at my knees with pain and guilt.

The word God will appear in my writings. I hope that doesn't scare you. These are not religious narratives, but perhaps you will notice, as have I, a certain power or force or spirituality that follows my ramblings.

I call it coincidence most of the time.

Draw your own conclusions.

It began sitting in a home, listening.

A slowness settling bones down to earth, roots and dirt, worms
and mushrooms anchoring attention in time.
No big deal, she said—just aliveness sensing itself—pulsing,
warm, the sun unable to keep up with the snow.
No big deal—slow all the way down, search this body once
and for all for its soul. My mouth tasting all it wants. My feet
marching up muddy mountains.
No big deal narratives of conflict abound but so do those of
resolution.
You sat down head falling back laughing the black coffee in your
mug sloshing out onto you nightgown—*Do you see that ghost?*

Patterned light through closed lids is its own intelligence, No big deal.

The foundation is listening—this is how we learned to speak.
Mom and Dad pushing air from their lungs, vibrating cords in
their throats. Their own sandcastled perspectives given to us
through tone, inflection, rhythm.

This is how it works. No big deal.

We shape each other's soft, fleshy bodies with our words.

I slipped into the mystery

left the part of myself
that always has to know.

The me you knew
would have hated this
all mouth and tongue out wide

                                       not now.

I'm allowing everything

          arise
to   move

             fall

                       away.

I'm in a house

that is a mix of my current home,
North Heide Lane and Roosevelt Avenue.

I'm in my bed, Mom is in the hallway.

I follow her down the stairs
through the kitchen into a basement
and through the cellar door.

We're standing near a field that opens out onto the ocean.

She looks healthy, peaceful.
I ask if she is happy
about our writing.

She says yes and takes my hand.

The wind and waves pick up.
She's gone.
I can feel the aliveness of it all—

how we're all, it's all a process unfolding.

I feel connected to the process,
connected to my place in the lineage of mothers.
But mostly I'm glad I can finally feel her in my heart again.

Name the wildflowers, gather them gently for her:

Stickseeds sing violet—
know each other by touch,

Sulphur cinquefoil, pale yellow, delicate
find one another in an embrace

Sticky geranium—what are you, fuchsia? Checkerblooms?
Molecules bond, electrons share,

Chicory, sun-washed in purple and green
how strange we were taught the universe is sterile,

Showy goldeneye, like miniature sunflowers
certainly nothing exists in isolation

Pass by the paintbrushes—too explosive to pick
the imagined secular vessel broken

Common yarrow, Prairie sunflowers—soon taller than me
a terrible lie, this separation—

Leave the glacier lily—too soft to hold
ordered within narrow rules, is sky, is wind, is rain.

Silence

You and I are at our favorite spot—the sandy beach, at the lake near our home.

I watch you explore rocks, small bugs, dig, roll, kick and swim in the sand and water.

I feel transparent—my own inner space mixing effortlessly with the wind off the lake.

You barrel into me for a snuggle.

We sit in silence for a few moments.

I start to shift—gathering our belongs.

You grab my hand and say, "No, Momma, sit longer."

When we finally make it back to the car and you are safely bucked in, I start to put on our favorite playlist.

You quickly say, "No music Momma, the quiet feels good."

You're right. I turn the music off and roll down the windows.

The quiet today feels good.

ABOUT THE AUTHORS

Rebecca Brenner is a writer, journalist, and mindfulness meditation teacher. Her work has appeared in *TIME, the Los Angeles Times, Tin House,* and elsewhere. She serves as president and co-founder of Mindful. Summit County, a nonprofit devoted to mindfulness as a tool for community care, and is active in local LGBTQ+ advocacy and community-building efforts. *Paper House* is her debut memoir-in-verse—a personal reckoning with the intergenerational impact of addiction, loss, and the enduring bonds that continue.

Patricia Pearson spent over twenty years teaching English in the Diocese of Pittsburgh, where she shared her love of literature and the written word with heart and conviction. A proud member of Alcoholics Anonymous, she found meaning in sponsoring others and in the fellowship of recovery, even as she continued to face her own challenges with sobriety. The mother of five, Patricia was a woman of complexity, resilience, and deep feeling, whose presence, even in absence, remains woven into the lives she shaped and the stories she left behind.

At Wayfarer Books we believe poetry is the language of the earth. We believe words—shaped like rivers through wild places—can change the shape of the world. We publish poets and writers and renegades who stand outside of mainstream culture—poets, essayists, and storytellers whose work might withstand the scrutiny of crows and coyotes, those who are cryptic and floral, the crepuscular, and the queer-at-heart. We are more than just a publisher but a community of writers. Our mission is to produce books that can serve as a compass and map to all wayfarers through wild terrain.

wayfarerbooks.org